Wolves and Other Nightmares by Alicen Grey
© 2014 by Alicen Grey. All rights reserved.

No part of this book may be reproduced or transmitted in any form without express written permission from the author.

wolves and other nightmares
alicen grey

for all those people
   just like me

wolves and other nightmares
alicen grey

contents

trigger warning guide   5

beginning

genesis	9
follow the leader	11
seventeen	12
dee ehn ay	14
jove	15
papaver somniferum	16
lupine	18
wolves	19
a healing of the wounds of separation I	20
church	21
warning to myself back then	23
the invitation	24
hypnotist	25
(untitled)	26

being

let there be darkness	31
narcissistic contagion	32
and my name is an afterthought	35
feather	36
longing	39
that moment	41
altered in your absence	42
mindfucked	44
the real world	46

college 47
preoccupied 48
diagnosis 49

becoming

my mind went away yesterday 55
savior 56
dissociative 57
valley song 59
psycho-logic 60
voices 62
white noise 63
where i belong 65
starseed 66
carrion 67
claws 68
caved 69
anonymous 70
oracle 71
the funeral 72
a healing of the wounds of separation II 73

acknowledgments 75

about the author 77

trigger warning guide

This collection of poetry chronicles my spiritual journey during the past three years. Admittedly, it was not always a pleasant journey, and a few of the poems herein reflect that. Being mindful of anyone who is still learning to cope with the aftermath of their own traumatic experiences, I have decided to add "trigger warnings" to the poems whose subject matter may spark flashbacks, dissociative states, anxiety, or any other kind of traumatic response.

dissociation:
my mind went away yesterday (55), dissociative (57)

self-injury:
caved (69)

spiritual abuse:
let there be darkness (31), narcissistic contagion (32), mindfucked (44), diagnosis (49), psycho-logic (60)

These trigger warnings will also appear beneath the titles of each of these poems. But be cautioned: poetry is subject to personal interpretations, and triggers vary from person to person, so the trigger warnings I have provided may not suffice for everyone. If you are feeling especially sensitive, please read with care.

I wish you peace and healing on your own journey. Now, I invite you to glimpse into mine…

beginning

genesis

This story doesn't start with a beginning,
a nice "once upon a time"
or a "in a land far, far away."
This story starts
when I was 16.
This story starts
right here in my head
which isn't really *my* head anymore
—but we'll get to that.
This story starts
with a death
that looked like a birth
so no one would ask
any questions.

Grey-tinted skin and deteriorating frame
made me the perfect target
for your calculating, selenite
smile.
My self-destructive tendencies
rolled out the red carpet
for you to stifle my thoughts
in the guise of caring.

You were like the stories I'd written
you were like the daydreams I wove
out of my hair,
except you were real
and talking to me.

We danced like we were bowing down
to each other,
spoke for hours like we were
praying.

The more you gave me, the less I had
until my world was a translucent sheet of glass, shimmering,
halfway-reflecting, a window to your world, but fragile.
Crystallized air.

People like you should come with a warning label. One that reads,
"Worship at your own risk."

follow the leader

You are
the god of all things magnificent
a spider spinning stories
mangling life
lingering along the edges of my
ever-shrinking world
long after we've hung up
You are
the pressure building
around my edges
condensing my sense of identity
blurring me into She

She is
a goddess to which they fold over
and murmur reverent chants
a Queen for whom
they march and work
and march and work
She is
that girl with the mood-ring eyes
that girl who used telekinesis once
that girl who will kill them
if they don't believe her

They are
a school of fish
a swarm of bees
a herd of black sheep
saucer-eyed and desperate for her esoteric truths

They worship She
the way
She worships you.

seventeen

black no longer suits the
guitar-shaped figure of the
girl who is
what She wasn't
back then
thoughts and hair
no longer halt at her chin,
her limbs no more
retreat
at the kiss of soft, innocent
wind

for She is a new kind of pretty

wind chimes in her throat
emulate planets
in constant motion
and the whisper-thin
scarlet petals
of dream-giving flowers
catch the songs
like bowls collecting
water

stray felines become friends
sharing secrets so obscure
elephants roam as phantoms do
across her lucid plains

She dances along
a million arrow-paths at once
being helicoid
unpredictable
She feels from her stomach

and observes
with another eye

willows caress her cheek
mother Earth rocks her to sleep
forbidden creatures tempt her
from the deep

moths flicker at her borders
and leeches crave her crimson flood
but She understands
that the old kind of pretty
is over and done

dee ehn ay

my cells release themselves from me
break open at the touch, the bite
of harsh chemicals

this disconnect
this deconstruction
from my mouth to a plastic chalice
from there to a revealing vial
pierces my eyes with revelatory beauty:
    the entrails of my cells
    gather, unify
    their former-insides, currently-
        outsides
    join hands
    and I think I hear them singing

their filthy secrets
erupt from a mangled membrane
    split skin
    withered walls
    punctured pretty permanence
or so I thought

my life-giving ladders
my building blocks
a cloud of me

jove

"You sound like Jupiter," says the innocent shape of the little boy as he sweeps his gaze to the floor. I don't think he, with his short arms and stubby fingers, is aware of just how far he has plunged his grip into my chest. Silky translucent blankets of color billow down slow-motion over the fraction of the image of the boy looking dreamy and lost and oddly knowing. I wonder how he did that trick with his eyes turning into himself like that as he asked me why, why do you sound like Jupiter? And now I want to know why too. Here I go. I am reaching in now, palpating softly for the large orb, the grand sphere that is attached to me by many fine cords shooting out of my throat and through space, alive in the tones that resound in my mouth. It is out there, in here, like echoes travelling brilliantly outward only to return to the source. Spirals somehow. All things are spirals. And it makes my edges seem irrelevant, and this whole distance thing, illusory, because Jupiter's size and mystery lie right here in my tongue.

papaver somniferum

my children were small and green
I nursed them
from seeds to sprouts
in a rectangular box
packed with cheap soil
under the ceiling light
on my kitchen table

my children were humble,
voiceless
but they spoke in other ways

every morning, they called me
out of slumber
every afternoon, I would sit by them
tell them about my day
they listened
from down in their roots
every night, they took
dirt and light and breath
and laced together dreams
just for me

my children taught me
that brains and nerves
do not consciousness make
consciousness is a quality
shared between all lives
have you fingers
or flowers

I remember when they started dying
felt their death inside myself
a thirst of which I could not relieve them

though I gave everything I could
water, water, everywhere
and yet my skin, their skin
remained ever parched and wanting

finally, fatigue settled
like a brick to the bottom of a river
a lifeless body in its wake
my father churned the dirt,
covering their little green limbs
in ebony earth
I couldn't watch

diagnosis: root rot
a result of too much water,
too much love
I felt like a murderer

three years later
I cannot find
a love like the love
my poppies had for me,
their mother
or a connection
as deep as their roots
sunk into my chest

Wherever you are, my sleep-bringing flowers, I hope all is well with your souls.

lupine

so finely carved, as if in iron
each bristle a needle
each hair a thread
stiff, stone, metal coat

muscles woven from lunar light
braided-together ripples in a silver pond
luminescent waves of motion

silent witness, quiet eyes
guarded gaze
ocean throat, ghost mouth
space howl
filling craters in the moon
transcendent call

ice fog cloud phantom breath
stains the air between us
snow-reflecting irises
rest on me

they said: you are
so much like the wolf

wolves

incessant whine careens into
otherworldly arcs of sound
like the prism at the storm's end
but darker, icy, and I

dig my way through your layers
collecting dirty crescents
beneath my fingernails
I search, I search
for you

you hide from me
behind fur and frost,
wish for an end
isolate, silence and damage
yourself

they observe, the guardians
eyes noble obsidian
grins made of ivory, steel
they block the path that leads
us back

they bristle and tense
sinews tighten and
flex, a threat
you say, we'd better get out of here

but it's in your nerves, accept it
it's in your wrists and in your skull:
we were somewhere before this

defy them
reach out and touch the jaws in which Death sleeps

a healing of the wounds of separation I

the soul in my skin
desires union
the collision that
melts
flesh with flesh
the ancient dance preceding
creation, ecstasy

writhing in all things obscene
not-real, half-asleep
"make love to me"
I said to the
four-armed river-haired
dancing destroying
god

then there was
fire,
a ring of scathing heat
and in the center of it all:
our outlines
melding twisting merging
pure energy
no boundaries

forbidden lust for the divine
realized

church

The pastor's microphone moans in a ghostly manner, resounding inside the ribs like a rolling current or a whale under water.

Fish have jelly eyes & they go go go, darts, arrows with puckered lips, perpetually awaiting a salty kiss. I wonder what else they're waiting for.

They say god is love, but he sure hates an awful lot of things. They say he cares, but he's always turning the other cheek.

Back to fish: their scales are like armor, like waves, like the currents they pass through, like microcosmic reflections of their mother ocean.

I don't understand why he laughs at the prospect of god being in everything, and I don't understand why the congregation is laughing with him. Why do they revel in being disconnected? Why do they enjoy severing every thread that marks the way out of the labyrinth? Why do they worship distance & emptiness?

No wonder they look so blank. They can't remember where they came from. They can't see their reflection in the mountains — they only see an unattainable goal. They can't find their hearts in the stars — they only see a weak twinkle, a dying pulse.

dust air ocean tree valley sun moon stones spirals holes light dark earth world animal human flower wing claw whisker belly insect diamond mirror fern spiderweb breath cloud fog ice ember storm dream eye hand heart bone skin blood hair metal whisper space chasm: I am in them all.

Fish don't drink water, they inhabit it. They surround themselves with the ever-changing. In that, they become it. They don't merely put water into their bodies—they embody it. And they don't cry, because their eyes are forever water. There is no need for cleansing when you're perpetually renewed. They glide, allowing the flow to direct them.

I almost can't believe this lovely world of ideas has been hidden from me for so long.
Where the HELL was EYE?

warning to myself back then

Beware the water
whose still surface denies its depths.
Baptism is a lot like drowning.

Beware the fish
and the way its whole body
is shaped like an eye
like an I.

Beware the North star,
for when you follow it,
you follow the past.

Most of all,
beware the moment
fear becomes familiar.

the invitation

As I round the corner of Sinner Street,
and continue down Ascension Avenue,
I hear a murmur,
shady, toothy,
directed at me:
"Hey. Hey you."

Pause.

"Yeah, you."

I turn my head toward the source.
It's you, standing in a dark alley, face obscured by the brim of your hat.

Your mischievous grin
lights up the night
when you beckon:

"Wanna be a victim with me?"

hypnotist

I met a dangerous man today;
he did not tell me his name.
Most creatures would run at the sound of his steps
but I chose to become his prey.

His voice is the chill of snowfall
making icicles out of my screams.
His smile is the broken mirror I blame
for seven years of bad dreams.

I think that the moon balances in his palm
for he forms and alters the tides.
He pulls at the water in me, in me
and makes me like drowning alive.

I have tasted the dust that composes his bones,
I have flown on the winds of his breath,
I have seen with the light he takes from the sun
and it showed me he scavenges death.

This dangerous man is seducing me
into a choking embrace,
but I am content getting hurt, as long
as the hypnotist tells me I'm safe.

(untitled)

and on the thirteenth day
it culminated
into   a winding tree
          a winding tree
   with no mercy

being

let there be darkness
trigger warning: spiritual abuse

* It must acknowledge its origins.

the damaged beliefs
and jagged fault line of fangs
claws at my shoulder
lips at my ear

* It must succumb to demolition
as a flower curls to frost.

under your weight
your masked and shrouded form

* It must relinquish its face,
its reflection,
to allow yours to unfold and take throne.

gaping hole, echoes ricocheting along
tattered walls, screams, apologies, confessions, shame.

* It must expose its deepest crevices
to the wandering eyes
of the leader.

* It must obey.

narcissistic contagion
trigger warning: spiritual abuse

Look, you're the one who chose
to set me on this pedestal
then get down
on your knees
and keep your eyes below you
while your mouth
was aimed at me.
When the words that tumbled out
sounded awfully
ill-at-ease,
you
needed
me.

So, technically, it's your fault
that I did just what you asked:
I treated you like metal,
though you were thin as glass.
I aimed my holy fire
at the you behind the mask,
caused a major melt-down
hot iron, moving fast —
but you
wanted
that.

If you leave your skull wide open
don't expect
to keep your brain —
I mean, sorry, but your weakness
is getting
in my way.

Remember: when you worship
you assume the role of
slave.
Fuck your thoughts, fuck your words
who wants them
anyway?
When I'm ripping you to shreds
I'm the only thing that's
safe,
because I know you in and out
don't you see? We're both
the same.
What's the point of fighting?
It's only you that you
betray.
There's no way to run and hide
because the mirror makes me
stay
right here inside your chasm
right here inside your
shade.
I'm the shape of you, the outline
I'm the light that rusts and
frays
I'm the flood that overcomes you,
it's your space that I
invade
See, you can't keep God out, honey.
You can only hope and
pray
that I only leave a bruise, that
I won't make you bleed
today
that the hole I've ripped into you
at least lets in
brighter rays

or even, that it grows
and lets you leave me by
decay.
Oh wait, looks like you forgot:
I'm the reason you were
made.
I choose how you suffer
I choose how you
degrade.
You only choose how often
you fuck up and
disobey.

Okay?

Just let me reassure you
this glory's
worth the pain
so if you wanna glow like me,
well, you've gotta
play my game.
But there's only one rule
so there's no need
to be afraid:

When I ask you who you are,
you'd better say
my fucking name.

and my name is an afterthought

I am
starlight, long searching for recognition
the shimmer that dwells at the end of an eyelash
receding white noise you think you're still hearing
impending nightfall
      the sunset's ghost

I am
a reflection in a glass, walked past
the memories worms don't have about the sky
a flower's vague recollection
      of life underground

I am
a heart drawn in dripping ink
smudged mascara
the way a rain storm lingers in the air
      long after it ends

I am
stained glass cathedral windows, bleached by sun
my ankles after a day spent walking
children grown and parents alone
      wondering when this happened

I am
an afterthought
that's my name
it only occurs to you
      now.

feather

I imagine
feathers, pitch and unpleasant
escaping my grasp
reminding me of times
wings were things
that bent and folded
according to my will, carrying
dreams on lighter planes
and tearing down clouds from their glorious thrones
highlighted by a paranoid sunlight
and I am oh-so-aware
of size and its implications
of a small body teeming with bigger ideas
can't be expressed, can't be
let go of
I want to though

I imagine
a sky, rampaging against its boundaries
expanding to lengths the mind can't
curl itself around
though I try
to be all-pervasive, encompassing limits
transcending walls and ceilings
dangerous as that is
you see, eyes don't close because the light hurts
they close because
well, because
other worlds
invade that which we call the real

I imagine
a compendium of notes vibrating inside
the walls of my ear

shaking the house down
like a wolf's breath
hungry, guttural
eyes stray and find secrets amidst
the tremors of the body of
prey

can't shake that feeling of being hunted
off my fire-licked back
scorch marks entail
attempts at decomposition
futile, aimless tries at clarity
betray me in the form of ashes
fluttering off in the gentle wind
lifting my hair like an ebony crown
about my face
as tears find their way to my
gaping throat
singing
or something

but I imagine
music isn't melodious
in the way you'd expect
it is relentless, furious
growls from the belly of my
abandoned shell
my disrupted carcass
has so much to tell
I imagine
forever never
happened
and god was just a
grandiose girl
entranced with reflections in
the queen's chalice

on a card that told the future
or so they say

but it's
even more enticing
having never been born
all that potential
shifting for a starting point
too small to conceive of
light years beyond
is a memory, a dream
of something the clock has yet to reach
arms spinning madly
to line up with numbers
that set gears in motion
that lull me to sleep
a counterclockwise dream

I imagine
fingertips, silence, skeleton keys
shimmering, accidents, willow trees
foxes, beetles, dynasties
cosmic eggs, zeroes, water beads

I imagine,
one day
no more days.

longing

I crave you
like a dying star
expanding, mutilating
space and color
according to its lofty desire
for limit-
less-
ness.

I crave you
like a wounded thing
wallowing, allowing
a scarlet rush
to hollow,
to hush.

I crave you
like a starving heart,
rib-caged and
withering —
oh, look, I've
made room for you
where my body
used to be.

I crave you
like the darkness
craves the curious
and brave.
Its claws welcome you.
Come inside.

I crave you
like a rampant moth

lusts for light
for harsh, agonizing union.
flutter,
flutter,
bye.

that moment

bustling crowd uncertain of itself clogging halls and arteries congesting breathing patterns rushing to slow down and the movement becomes curious what's it like to interrupt oneself and the motion settles in a gradual fashion until I realize it was pulling back people-shaped curtains to reveal you standing there seeing me seeing you and the clock forgets its purpose and the world stops for the briefest most minute second moment breath blink and our faces might be moving unbeknownst to us attempting the sweet giddy smiles that used to adorn us or maybe the confused awkward longing I feel you feel it too that keeps us both awake sometimes and I watch your lips pull back like your brain is maneuvering the strings and your eyes glisten why why and suddenly the world is moving again and we understand why our hearts are in pieces on the floor

altered in your absence

it's a good thing you turned around
as my robe went hush to the ground
and fell in a rush to the wooden slats that supported
my twisted ankles
also falling
I was calling
your name

it's a good thing you left when you did
door clicked shut on the back of your head
knob waited for my wrist
to come and twist
and follow
but now I'm glad
I ignored it

oh, mister man with the hands
you and your fickle plans
oh, mister you-with-the-teeth
you do not scare me
no, no

it's a good thing you weren't there
to watch me dismantle and regroup and repair
and finally stand on my own,
knees shaking, then stone
remembering you, then grown
the near-dead bulb drawing out my golden undertones
and casting shadows alongside my curves
distorting the way I assemble and swerve
luscious-untouched
actually-touched-once
or twice
or thrice

but pure, somehow
and better now
that you're not here to hear me sing
and that sliver between my legs is more of a smile
than anything

oh mister-man-with-the-bones
it was all for show
oh mister man-with-the-mind
I have my own

so, go

mindfucked

trigger warning: spiritual abuse

I
it all comes together in hazy swirls
me, there, in bed
arms draped about my head
drifting languidly, laggardly
between two worlds
that aren't really separate
anyway

my world:
the palace, the temple of a goddess named She, a replica of
your world:
labyrinthine, nightmarish and all I've ever wanted—
but here we are, unraveling

(everyone secretly wants to be owned)

for hours
you twist and distort
every word, every thought
every thing I dare to call mine
for hours
you claw and shred your way through my layers,
gutting me, coring me,
until I am hollowed remains
struggling for breath
and then you sit back and laugh
as I try to figure out
who the hell just broke into me

II
god is not benevolent
I don't care what you've been told
listen to me
listen to me

god can kill
and he does

the real world

Okay, She-goddess, that's enough — come down from there this instant! There's no time for fooling around anymore. You were supposed to be at The Real World by now. Oh, stop whining. Put your shoes on – adults don't walk around barefoot. Wash that fairy dust off your face and comb the spider webs out of your hair. If you hadn't been reading those silly magic books of yours, you wouldn't be so late! You have to read real books from now on. No more Aleister Crowley for you, young lady. Now pack your things — oohhhhh no, no no *no*, not *those* things. You leave those crystals and tarot cards here. There's no time for them. When you enter The Real World you have to leave those behind. Stop dilly-dallying, you'll miss the next train! What are you, seventeen? Do I have to do everything for you? Stop crying, right now. There's no time for crying. Where you're going, time is money. People who waste their time crying end up poor. Do you want to be poor? Here, let's me help you pack. You're going to need a metro card, money, a job, a sense of direction, a backbone, an attitude, a middle finger, more money… No, you cannot bring your sense of higher purpose with you. Quit horsing around, you've got work to do and people to please and dreams to give up on! Hurry up! Now don't forget: if you need anything, just call. I'll always be here to remind you that you are useless. The Real World is not a nice place but at least it pays the bills— here comes your train. Have fun!

college

The Real World is a place where they laugh at you
because you're just another freshman:
a small brown girl with a high-pitched voice
kind of like a mosquito
before someone
slams a palm down
on its existence.

preoccupied

She called me a few times
I didn't answer right away
because I was in an important meeting
and I figured She could wait
when I called her back
She told me
we need to talk
so I pulled out my planner
found a slot for her
between a dress rehearsal and poli-sci
thinking half an hour would be enough time
to talk to the goddess
we met up in a coffee shop
right away I said
I might have to cut this short
because I have class soon—
She said
She was going away
to go be a goddess
somewhere else
wait
no
She wasn't allowed to
up and leave me like that
was She?
I wanted to ask her where She was going
I wanted her to invite me along
but by the time I realized it
She was already gone
and I was only talking to myself

There wasn't even time to say goodbye.

diagnosis

trigger warning: spiritual abuse

I read a book about us, about our "friendship"
(or whatever the hell that shit was)
written by a pair of psychologists
who were trying to help people to not-die
which is nice of them and all, but
I read it a few years too late

Chapter 1: Characteristics Of A Soul-Eater
Check all that apply:
- ☐ this person reads your thoughts
- ☐ this person uses their psychic powers against you
- ☐ this person died and was resurrected
- ☐ this person knows everything in the whole universe
- ☐ this person can kill things by willing them to die
- ☐ this person has an all-seeing eye
- ☐ this person is watching you from miles away
- ☐ this person will punish you on a cosmic scale if you don't do what they tell you to do
- ☐ this person is god
- ☐ this person is not a cult leader

Chapter 2: How To Know If You Live In a Cage
- ☐ you actually believe this person can read your thoughts
- ☐ you actually believe this person has psychic powers
- ☐ you actually believe this person died and was resurrected
- ☐ you actually believe this person knows everything in the whole universe
- ☐ you actually believe this person can kill things by willing them to die
- ☐ you actually believe this person has an all-seeing eye

- ☐ you actually believe this person is watching you from miles away
- ☐ you actually believe this person will punish you on a cosmic scale if you don't do what they tell you to do
- ☐ you actually believe this person is god
- ☐ you actually believe this person is not a cult leader

Chapter 3: How You Feel Upon Exiting the Cage
- ☐ like the entire world no longer makes sense
- ☐ like everything is now suspect
- ☐ like none of my thoughts are mine anymore
- ☐ like anything I believe is going to kill me
- ☐ like my reality just collapsed in on itself and now there's nothing nothing nothing nothing nothing

Chapter 4: How to Cope With Freedom
- ☐ don't

becoming

my mind went away yesterday
trigger warning: dissociation

I
My mind went away yesterday,
and it's nowhere to be found.
I could tell you I feel
numb,
but if I'm numb
how do I know
what I'm feeling?

I could tell you this is like
a desert with no sand,
a void ocean.
But those words have weight
and there is no substance here.
There is no "here."

I can't even say I'm alone because
alone means
being by one's self
but there is no being,
there is no one,
and there is no self.

II
God, are you still there?

III
...God?

savior

you found me after the world collapsed
a heap of exhaustion and defeat,
each breath an attempt to stay alive
leaned down,
checked my pulse
there's still hope

you told me,
We look the same. We got hurt the same.
We grew up here. Me, you. The same moon hangs in both our skies,
and the sun wandered off a long time ago trying to find something
it never had, and the trees around here whisper and weep, and the
wind and the rain know too much, and the ground shakes and
heaves sometimes like it's screaming, screaming, and that's the only
lullaby you're ever gonna get.

Do you trust me?

then, you
slid your palms
beneath my weight
lifted me
up

I've never felt so high
in my life

dissociative
trigger warning: dissociation

cavernous hollow in my skull
depleted chasm left behind
in the wake of my mind
ripped from reality
no warning, no weapon or shield,
absolute silence inside my own head
not a thought,
not one single thought
      for days

walking this earth with no sense of direction
all my most familiar places became
foreign, strange, surreal
suspicious of lampposts
distrustful of grass
sorry, I
don't know what a sidewalk is
stared at something today
for two minutes
before I figured out
      it's a dog

crushing grief
spiritual death
used to be god
did you hear me
I used to be god
and now I'm
well
      look at me

sorrow so ruthless
mind ejects from its vessel

can't cope, can't grasp it
    I can't pretend to be here anymore

said nothing to family
said little to friends
instead, spoke to bright white rectangular lights
late at night,
looking for reasons and answers
reassurance
that I am not the only one
comfort, relief, someone to hold me,
    I'll take anything

"Be in the present moment,"
they tell me
and I would be
if only I knew
    where I was

valley song

these veins are threatening me
these irises carry too much
salt rivers running, cutting even stone
mood rings faded, blinked and broke a bone

these wrists remember my name
these ribs, they almost forgot
skeleton screaming, better stay below
heartbeat whispers, maybe you should go

these legs are daring themselves
to follow the memory out
lips too eager, talking in my sleep
about a girl, or something like a dream

these hands are curious, grieving
these ears are waiting on signs
maybe the valley will end when I wake
maybe the mountain was just a mistake

but the looking glass torments its voyeur
and she obeys, as she always has
and the throat, wide open, makes not a sound
and the goddess, lofty, floats back down

a fault line adorns my chest
a wound, or maybe a window
but here we are, not seeing
what a dissonant way of being

psycho-logic
trigger warning: spiritual abuse

perfumed with the
contents of your
veins

entitled to
horrors of your
fame

privileged to
bow and chant your
name

anointing that
looks more like a
stain

abandoned but
couldn't leave your
throne

pinnacle of
all I'd ever
known

secret prayer
under my breath be-
stowed

with every fear you
etched into my
home

words connect but
hollow, wither,
spin

framework fucked and
girl lost trust with-
in

countless times the
fish just couldn't
swim

if only she could
give it to the
wind

gaping wounds that
nobody can
see

tombstone where a
memory should
be

psycho-logic
yet nostalgic,
me

tell me, is this
what they meant by
"free"?

voices

I could sing
the way church bells cast their resonance so far and reverberate
along the round surfaces of the jewel-tone orbs that dangle like
ornaments in the vast expanse we call outer-space that is really just
a hologram.

I could sing
the way tawny gritty sand mountains inch forward like patient
elders crossing dry ruthless scorching dunes that crawl like I did
back to you every time making excuses giving reasons when I knew
I shouldn't have defended you.

I could sing
the way whales trumpet long and far to find each other across
barren hollow oceans of turbulence and sorrow that reflect what is
happening in me, no one else can hear, no one else can hear.

I could sing I'm sorry
I could sing You were right
I could sing Please come back

I would sing,
but when you vanished
my voice vanished too.

white noise

all the tragedies befallen
rings slipping off fingers
friends too far away *too close*

pressure imprinting little tiny words
onto marble-pearly paper
I've never borne a blankness so profound,
so much to say, fail to make a sound

I owe the words to outsiders with
reminders in all the same places
mechanical, taking part in society
hair veiling all sorts of things
tiny painful
burning things

I owe the words to all those people
just like me

instead: formidable silence
the residue of a story
with stream-of-consciousness rivers
drying up between the lines
there goes my mind
the phantasm chalk outline
of a garden once-thrived
now one bold red faced flower struggles to speak my name

I could once find words for
anything, lacing sonic shapes
together via meaningful patterns
effortless strokes forging memories
we collectively share, wishes we

haphazardly clutch, chanting
graceful ink-stained soliloquies
flowflowing from lithe wrists

but then this
happened

I have yet to find forgiveness
for this not-knowing what to say
for this mindless passing of days
for this…
whatever this is

Years.
Finally, trying to articulate
all these years.
Delicately coaxing thoughts out of
hiding places, maybe even
begging a little:
please, please find a form.
But when I lift my pen
away from the paper
the epitaph
the only chance we all had
of being understood—

I find there,
white noise,
nothing at all.

where i belong

not in the soft forgiving arms of the willow tree,
not in the healing sands of time,
not in the redeeming river,
not in the gentle unfurling of petals opening up to receive light,
not in the ebb and flow of the ocean,
not in the sway of the candle flame,
not in the breaths I take between words, and not in the words themselves,
not in the paranoia of the waking world,
not in the liquid black silk of night that billows down like a curtain to hide me away,
not in the shining celestial bodies that invite mine to come out of hiding,
not in the dreams that devastate,
not in the dreams that bring you back to me,
not in the opening of eyes that means it wasn't real,
not in the monotonous way life continues,
not in the questions, not in the answers,
not in the fact that I don't pray anymore,
not in the uncertain steps I call dancing,
not in the shadow that mocks my every move,
not in the scars that adorn my outer layers,
not in the scars that adorn my inner layers,
not in the fading after-image of what came before me
not in what is to come,
not in my shell, not in my reflection, not in my clothes, not in my house, not on my street, not in my head, not in my chest, not in my hands, not in your arms, not in mine,
so where?

starseed

I had a dream last night:

My soul was suspended in a vast stretch of deep pink galaxy: behemoth planets hummed from down in their bellies. Stars shimmered and shone like frozen diamonds. I, body, viewed from a distance as my soul basked in their mighty presence.

A voice pierced the scene, urgent, concerned, "Why won't you come back?"
The voice was coming from Earth.

My soul replied,
"Because I just...
I just want to go home, okay?"

carrion

when it's over,
>I'll be a hardened corpse
>on the street that once was a river
>under the trees I never knew
>in a frenzy of lights and noise, lights and noise
>still in the midst of never-ending motion
>acclimating
>or trying to

when we're done,
>I'll be where the night never stops
>cradling a bruise
>that's shaped like you
>wondering why sleep
>never came to me
>wondering how
>I still dreamed

when you need me,
>I'll be polluted, inhaling fumes
>in a cold hard city
>dirty ugly sad, sad city
>waiting for change

when you find me,
>don't stop
>carry on

claws

They warned me about boys like you.
Only polite when you benefit.
Sweet until you get what you want.
Then suddenly your hugs become transparent and your eyes glint
like knives and my, what big claws you have.
All the better to break my heart with, I guess.

It was no accident
when I floated off the dance floor
and onto the couch beside you
bared my soul to your undeserving ears,
cried and cried while you considered
your next move.

Don't be fooled: I did not need you.
I just needed –
needed, like water or oxygen –
someone to hold me.
I was hollow and lost and afraid and you're not the only one
capable of using people, okay?

One moment on your lap,
one moment of penetrating warmth,
one moment of human contact,
one moment where we both wondered, our lips mere inches apart,
if this would become our excuse
to go too far.

And then I pulled away.

Yeah, they warned me about boys like you.
But they clearly didn't warn you
about girls like me.

caved

trigger warning: self-injury

When the mechanical husk walked by,
someone told it,
"You really look tired. You should get some rest."

When the vacant shell sat by a window and somberly contemplated life,
a passerby joked at it:
"Did somebody die?"

When the dry chalky skeleton mumbled on the phone,
its parents pleaded,
"Why are you so sad?"

When the fading outline almost broke into tears in class five times,
its classmates politely turned away.

When the ugly useless annoying waste of space asked the nice lady at the store if they had any Saint John's Wort because it thinks it's depressed, the nice lady waved to it on its way out and sheepishly said, "I hope you feel better."

But when the vanishing act realized that happy pills were not enough, it caved into temptation and got itself a new pack of razors and exposed its thigh and carved little red lines of defiance into its cold, cold skin, laid back on the carpet, savored the warmth of the wounds, and breathed in.

anonymous

to a ring of anonymous faces
at a meeting I found out about
on the Internet
during one of my desperate information-hunts
for people like me
so I wouldn't feel alone anymore,
I made a confession

but this ring of anonymous faces
did not laugh
they did not shrug
or doubt me
or get annoyed
or change the subject
or call me stupid and wrong and overdramatic

instead, the ring of anonymous faces
nodded
solemnly, kindly,
as if to say,
"We understand."

and just like that,
the ring of anonymous faces
became a circle of friends

oracle

I looked for truth in the faces of cards,
I looked for wealth by flipping six coins,
I looked for myself in a crystal ball,
I looked for love in magic potions,
I looked for friends in yoga classes,
I looked for confidence in pretty stones,
I looked for health in Sanskrit chants,
I looked for faith in New Age books,
I looked for wisdom in neon signs that flashed the words PSYCHIC
    READINGS ONLY $10
and then I realized
these are things you can only find
within.

the funeral

Once upon a time,
I was the goddess named She.

She was
a being made of Light
the Ocean incarnate
Jupiter's voice.
She was
the daughter of Shiva
a friend to the Wolves
and other nightmares.

Once upon a time,
I was alive.
That was before god killed the goddess,
before the fish and the bees and the black sheep
moved on without me,
before the poppies died and my eyes stopped
changing colors.
A few years later, the Winter came.

With a candle and a prayer,
I wrote her name down,
told her I loved her,
and tucked her away in a furrow of earth.

But now it's Spring again, and
there's a new consciousness growing
in the spot where She lay:
a tree, with leaves of dark green.

Imagine if you hadn't found me.

a healing of the wounds of separation II

the space between us, a wound
even a breath away, too great a distance

but now:
bodies entwine like cosmic serpents
cascading onto the mattress
tangle of skin and need
collision of me and you

now:
every thrust closes the distance
every touch, every kiss dulls the ache
as oceans part
and a rush of foaming waves
weaves through me like white rivers

now:
vortex, spinning wildly open
lotus petals bursting outward
like the points
of a searing hot star

now:
revolutions happening in my core
turning counterclockwise
winding back through all these years
5, 4, 3
2 hearts

now:
one

acknowledgements

Mary, my soul sister: It is a precious experience to become completely vulnerable to someone and not have to regret it later. Thank you for listening without judgment.

Amanda: You have borne witness to every stage of this dream-turned-nightmare-turned-awakening, and your presence has remained constant. Thank you for sticking with me.

Roman: You saw me struggling to make sense of my world, and you stopped to help me up. You cared enough to make sure that I, almost a complete stranger to you at the time, was okay. Your emails, advice, phone calls and encouraging words have been more instrumental to my healing process than anything else, and I will never be able to thank you enough for your selflessness.

To that certain group of people that meets on a certain day of the month: thank you for existing. I don't know that I would be stable now, had I not found you when I did. It's comforting to know I'm not alone.

To everyone else I haven't mentioned by name: you know who you are, and you know that I love you.

about the author

Alicen Grey has been writing since the age of six. In 2011, she won first place in the esteemed Rebecca Marie Aronson writing competition. She is also the recipient of numerous writing awards, including the Lisa See Snow Flower and The Secret Fan Excellence in Writing Award. She currently lives in Mount Vernon, New York, and attends Hunter College as a creative writing major. This is her first collection of poetry.

www.ingramcontent.com/pod-product-compliance
Lightning Source LLC
LaVergne TN
LVHW020938090426
835512LV00020B/3410